SIDNEY WICKS

BILL WALTON

DAMON STOUDAMIRE

DAVE TWARDZIK

CLYDE DREXLER

RASHEED WALLACE

JEROME KERSEY

BUCK WILLIAMS

MAURICE LUCAS

ARVYDAS SABONIS

KIKI VANDEWEGHE

SCOTTIE PIPPEN

THE HISTORY OF THE PORTLAND TRAIL BLAZERS
CREATIVE EDUCATION
AARON FRISCH

Published by Creative Education, 123 South Broad Street, Mankato, MN 56001

Creative Education is an imprint of The Creative Company.

Designed by Rita Marshall

Photos by Allsport, AP/Wide World, NBA Photos, SportsChrome

Library of Congress Cataloging-in-Publication Data

Frisch, Aaron. The history of the Portland Trail Blazers / by Aaron Frisch.

p. cm. – (Pro basketball today) ISBN 1-58341-111-9

1. Portland Trail Blazers (Basketball team)–History–

Juvenile literature. [1. Portland Trail Blazers (Basketball team)–History.

2. Basketball–History.] I. Title. II. Series.

GV885.52.P67 F75 2001 796.323'64'0979549–dc21 00-047332

First Edition 9 8 7 6 5 4 3 2 1

NEARLY 200 YEARS AGO, EXPLORERS MERIWETHER LEWIS AND WILLIAM CLARK BLAZED A TRAIL ACROSS the untamed American West. Their epic journey, which ended in the Pacific Northwest, opened the way for pioneers. In 1845, some of these pioneers set up a trading post at the junction of the Columbia and Willamette Rivers, and the city of Portland was born.

Portland, Oregon, has since grown to more than 400,000 people. Known as the "City of Roses"—due to its many public and private rose gardens—Portland is renowned for its natural beauty. Since 1970, the city has also been known for its National Basketball Association (NBA)

GEOFF PETRIE

team. In honor of the brave explorers who put Portland on the map, that team was named the Portland Trail Blazers.

The Trail Blazers won their first game in franchise history, beating Cleveland 115–112.

{A SLOW START} The Trail Blazers' home court was Memorial Coliseum, an arena with about 12,000 seats. Only about half of those seats were filled for the first few seasons, however. Like most teams just starting out, the Trail Blazers lost a lot of games.

Even though Blazers fans saw few victories, they were able to watch two special players—sharpshooting guard Geoff Petrie and versatile forward Sidney Wicks. Portland used its first selection in the 1970 NBA Draft to select Petrie. He quickly earned a reputation as a deadly shooter, sometimes scoring more than 40 points per game.

Wicks joined Portland after helping to lead the University of California at Los Angeles (UCLA) Bruins to the college national champi-

SCOTTIE PIPPEN

Sidney Wicks averaged nearly 24 points and 11 rebounds per game in **1972–73**.

SIDNEY WICKS

onship in both 1969 and 1970. At 6-foot-9 and 225 pounds, Wicks was big enough to play center and quick enough to play small forward. His versatility soon earned him a nickname among Portland fans: "Mr. Everything."

But as good as they were, Petrie and Wicks couldn't lead the Trail Blazers to a winning record. In fact, Portland finished the 1973–74 season with a 27–55 record—the worst in the Western Conference. Fortunately, the weak record gave the Trail Blazers the top pick in the 1974 NBA Draft. To no one's surprise, Portland used the pick to select a towering, redheaded center named Bill Walton.

In **1973–74**, guard Larry Steele led the NBA in steals with almost three per game.

Like Wicks, Walton had played college ball at UCLA. Even though Walton was 6-foot-11 and could score seemingly at will, he was also a great passer. Basketball experts predicted that he would turn even the

LARRY STEELE

With the addition of Bill Walton, the struggling Blazers were transformed into champions.

BILL WALTON

worst NBA team around. Portland fans expected nothing less.

{WORLD CHAMPIONS} Unfortunately, Walton didn't make the Blazers into winners in his first two seasons. Sidelined with various injuries, he played in only about half of the team's games. Without their center, the Blazers continued to struggle, and Lenny Wilkens—the team's first head coach—was fired.

High-rising forward Lloyd Neal swatted away nearly two shots per game in **1975–76**.

Jack Ramsay took over as coach in 1976. Portland also featured a new lineup that year. Petrie and Wicks had both been traded, and the Blazers' new starting lineup consisted of guards Dave Twardzik and Lionel Hollins, forwards Maurice Lucas and Bobby Gross, and a healthy Walton in the middle.

Ramsay demanded that his team play aggressive defense and unselfish offense. No player did both better than Walton, who was final-

JACK RAMSAY

ly free of injury and able to play his best. “For two years, I wasn’t able to run up and down the court freely without . . . thinking about [my injuries],” Walton explained. “That’s no way to play basketball.”

Behind their big center, the Trail Blazers raced up the standings. They made the playoffs for the first time after the 1976–77 season, then battled past Chicago and Denver to reach the Western Conference

Finals. There they faced the Los Angeles Lakers, who were also led by a dominant center: Kareem Abdul-Jabbar. Walton got the better of the matchup as the Blazers swept the series in four games.

Maurice Lucas and Bill Walton combined to grab 25 rebounds per game in **1976–77**.

Portland next took on the Philadelphia 76ers for the NBA championship. Led by stars "Dr. J" (Julius Erving) and George McGinnis, Philadelphia won the first two games. But something happened late in game two that would turn the series' momentum around. Maurice Lucas and 76ers center Darryl Dawkins got into a short but spectacular fight. Dawkins was a powerful player, but "Big Mo" proved that he was not intimidated.

Inspired by Lucas's tenacity, the Blazers rebounded to win the next three games. In game six, with only seconds left and Portland ahead 109–107, Philadelphia's McGinnis drove to the basket and lofted the ball up. Walton was there for the block, however, swatting the ball

DALE DAVIS

HEALTH NET
BLAZERS
34
BLAZERS

back to midcourt. The horn then sounded as Portland fans raced onto the floor to celebrate their first NBA title.

The next day, 50,000 people lined the streets of downtown

Portland for a victory parade. They had the best team in the league, and one of the youngest as well. "Blazermaniacs" were sure that Walton—the league's Most Valuable Player—would lead Portland to glory again.

{CLYDE GLIDES TO STARDOM} The next season, the Trail Blazers raced to an incredible 50–10 record before Walton suffered a broken foot. Without their center, the Blazers finished 58–24 and lost in the first round of the playoffs.

If Blazers fans were disappointed by the loss, they were stunned a few months later. Walton, who felt that the Portland medical staff had not treated his injury properly, announced that he wanted to be traded. The Blazers eventually sent the big redhead to the San Diego Clippers. Sadly, nagging injuries would prevent Walton from ever becoming a full-time star again.

Versatile guard Dave Twardzik was a steady presence in Portland throughout the late **'70s**.

Even without Walton, the Blazers remained competitive. Such outstanding players as center Mychal Thompson, forward Calvin Natt, and guard Jim Paxson emerged to lead the Blazers to winning records over the next few years. Still, they struggled to find playoff success again.

DAVE TWARDZIK

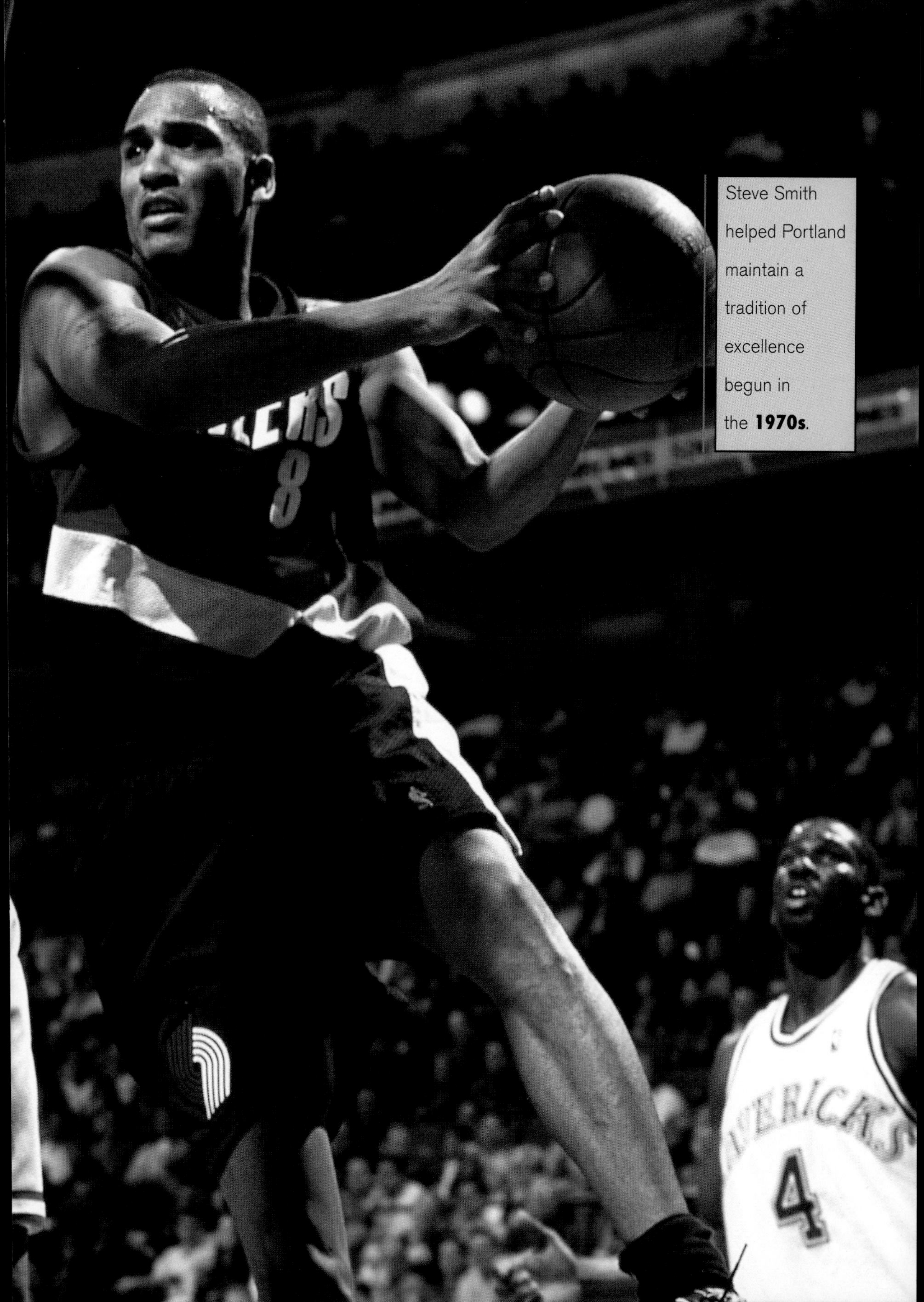

Steve Smith helped Portland maintain a tradition of excellence begun in the **1970s**.

In 1984, the Blazers tried shaking things up by trading several players to the Denver Nuggets for forward Kiki Vandeweghe. Not the fastest or most athletic player on the court, Vandeweghe instead used his intelligence to become a feared scorer. "He [the defender] is always going to make a mistake—leaning the wrong way, too close, the wrong foot forward, shifting his eyes," he once explained. "You just have to wait for his mistake and capitalize on it."

Forward Kiki Vandeweghe averaged more than 22 points per game in his first three seasons in Portland.

Led by Vandeweghe and a young shooting guard named Clyde Drexler, the Blazers led the league in scoring in 1986–87. The next season, they finished with a 53–29 record. Vandeweghe struggled with back problems that year, but Drexler more than picked up the slack. Mike Schuler, who had just replaced Ramsay as head coach, knew he had a rising star. "The fans are only now coming to realize the kind of

KIKI VANDEWEGHE

player we have in Clyde," Schuler said.

When Portland selected him out of the University of Houston in the 1983 NBA Draft, Drexler was known as a great jumper but an aver-

age shooter, passer, and defender. But Drexler, known as "Clyde the Glide" because of his smooth moves and great vertical leap, soon showed he could do it all.

Drexler scored plenty of points throughout the late 1980s, but the Blazers lost in the playoffs every year. In 1989, Portland made a coaching change, promoting assistant Rick Adelman. The new coach knew his team had plenty of potential. Forward Jerome Kersey and center Kevin Duckworth formed a burly inside combination, while point guard Terry Porter helped Drexler move the ball. By trading for hardworking power forward Buck Williams, the Blazers had the makings of a true contender.

Kevin Duckworth played in the **1991** All-Star Game alongside Clyde Drexler and Terry Porter.

{GLORY YEARS AGAIN} This new lineup returned Portland to glory. In 1989–90, the Blazers went 59–23 and drove all the way to the NBA Finals. Although they lost the championship to the Detroit Pistons, they came back stronger and more determined the next season.

After adding Danny Ainge and Walter Davis—a pair of great

KEVIN DUCKWORTH

Guard Clyde Drexler thrilled Portland fans with his high-flying heroics for 12 seasons.

CLYDE DREXLER

BLAZERS
52

outside shooters—to their lineup, the Blazers started the year 19–1 and finished with a 63–19 record. In the playoffs, they battled as far as the Western Conference Finals, where they fell to the Lakers in six games. "We're a better team than we showed," Drexler said after the series. "We'll be back."

Buck Williams led the Blazers in rebounding as they made two NBA Finals appearances.

Drexler backed up his promise, averaging 25 points per game the next year and leading Portland on one more run at the NBA championship. In the playoffs, Portland crushed Los Angeles, Phoenix, and Utah to reach the Finals again. The Blazers' opponent this time was the Chicago Bulls, led by superstar Michael Jordan. Although Portland fought valiantly, Jordan proved to be too much as the Bulls triumphed in six games.

Sadly, the Blazers began to slide down the standings in the seasons that followed. Many of the team's top players—including Duckworth,

BUCK WILLIAMS

Kersey, and Porter—were traded away, and injuries began to slow Drexler down.

One of the brightest spots during those years was forward Cliff

Robinson. The 6-foot-10 Robinson, easily recognized by the headband he wore around his shaved dome, had great speed and a soft shooting touch. He emerged as a true star in 1993–94, averaging more than 20

points a game and representing Portland in the All-Star Game.

Robinson remained a steady presence, but 1995 brought three major changes. P.J. Carlesimo replaced Rick Adelman as coach, the Blazers played their final games in Memorial Coliseum, and Drexler was traded to the Houston Rockets. It was the end of an era.

Jerome Kersey became just the second player to grab 5,000 rebounds in a Blazers uniform.

{STARTING OVER} With Drexler gone, Portland needed a new anchor around which to rebuild. The team found that player in Arvydas Sabonis, a 7-foot-3 center from Lithuania. Portland had drafted Sabonis in 1986, but he had decided to play in Europe instead. Finally, nearly a decade later, he brought his unique abilities to Portland.

Sabonis was a skilled rebounder and scorer and was even known to launch three-pointers with amazing accuracy. But what really made him special was his passing ability. Sabonis could flip the ball behind his back

JEROME KERSEY

or fire full-court passes with the skill of a point guard. "Arvydas and Bill Walton are the two best passing big men ever," said Milwaukee coach Mike Dunleavy. "No one else is even close."

Versatile big man Arvydas Sabonis connected on 49 three-point shots in **1996–97**.

Paul Allen, the Blazers' wealthy owner, was willing to pay top dollar to surround Sabonis with outstanding players. In 1996, Allen and his staff brought in guards Kenny Anderson and Isaiah Rider and fiery forward Rasheed Wallace. Although all three players had great talent, they also had earned reputations as troublemakers with their disruptive behavior on and off the basketball court.

This talented but inexperienced lineup played erratically, beating the NBA's elite teams one night and losing to the worst clubs the next. Still, Portland fans were happy with the rebuilding process. The Blazers were exciting to watch again, and the team boasted a fabulous new home

ARVYDAS SABONIS

court—the 20,000-seat Rose Garden in downtown Portland.

{BLAZING TO THE TOP} In 1998–99, Portland emerged as one of the NBA's heavyweights again under new coach Mike Dunleavy. Newly acquired point guard Damon Stoudamire ran a fast-paced offense, Rider and Wallace led a balanced scoring attack, and Sabonis and muscular forward Brian Grant controlled the boards as the Blazers went 35–15 and won two playoff series.

Forward Brian Grant provided much of Portland's low-post power in the late **'90s**.

After the season, Portland made its most aggressive move yet, trading for All-Star guards Scottie Pippen and Steve Smith. In Chicago, the 6-foot-7 Pippen had teamed up with Michael Jordan to lead the Bulls to six NBA championships. The Blazers were thrilled to add his experience and well-known defensive prowess to their lineup. "He's the best defender I've seen," said Coach Dunleavy. "Jordan, at his position, may have been

BRIAN GRANT

Forward Rasheed Wallace led the Trail Blazers with his strong inside play and intensity.

RASHEED WALLACE

Point guard Damon Stoudamire led Portland deep into the playoffs once again in **2000**.

DAMON STOUDAMIRE

as good as there was. But Scottie could guard more positions . . . [and] handle more sizes."

Portland added to its frontcourt in **2000–01** by trading for All-Star forward Shawn Kemp.

Portland made the playoffs for the 19th straight season in 1999–00, then battled to a Western Conference Finals showdown with the Los Angeles Lakers. Star center Shaquille O'Neal led the Lakers to a three-games-to-one series lead, but the Blazers battled back, winning the next two. Unfortunately, Portland then blew a 15-point lead late in the deciding game seven to lose the series.

Though the defeat was heartbreaking, the Blazers remain more determined than ever to capture that elusive second NBA title. And with their deep and talented roster, championship glory is certainly within reach. As Portland general manager Bob Whitsitt said, "We've seen the top of the mountain. Now we're trying to plant the flag."

SHAWN KEMP